The
Hang Gliding
Book

The Hang Gliding Book

William Bixby

Technical adviser: Keith Nichols,
U.S. National Hang Gliding Champion,
1976

David McKay Company, Inc.
New York

Illustration credits: All photographs in this book by Bettina Gray except for
the following: p. 12. Smithsonian Institution, negative #A-42.413-c; p. 14.
Smithsonian Institution, negative #A-48095-L. Drawings by George
Shortmeier.

Library of Congress Cataloging in Publication Data
Bixby, William.
The hang gliding book.

1. Hang gliding—Juvenile literature. I. Title.
GV764.B5   797.5'5   77-5227
ISBN 0-679-20428-8

10 9 8 7 6 5 4 3 2 1

Manufactured in the United States of America

Contents

1. Flying Like a Bird   1
2. The Birth of Hang Gliding   9
3. How Gliders Fly   19
4. Glider Country, Glider Winds   29
5. The Danger in Hang Gliding   43
6. Competition   57
7. New Gliders and Tomorrow   71

The
Hang Gliding
Book

1
Flying Like a Bird

From the earliest time, men have envied the freedom of birds in flight. In fact, we often use a phrase that says just that: "free as a bird."

Today, more and more people are experiencing that freedom in the sport of hang gliding. From the coastal cliffs and mountains of California to the shores of Cape Cod in Massachusetts, these "free-as-a-bird" fliers are launching their gliders. They use no motors, only the wind. Once their gliders are launched, the fliers must use all their skill, knowledge, and luck to stay in the sky, make a successful flight, and land safely. Some flights last for hours. Others last only a few minutes. But all who fly say they have never felt so free and peaceful before.

One veteran flier, Charles Baughman, gets his greatest kick soaring with eagles. While flying, he often has eagles maneuver alongside of him. They eye him curiously as he imitates them, and, for a moment, he feels as if he *is* an eagle. Then, with

A pilot launches his
glider over the
California coast.

greater skill than Baughman possesses, the eagles
soar far above him and disappear from view.

Even beginners find their first few seconds in the
air an unforgettable experience. David Reed, of
Vermont, is a beginner. He takes his glider to a
small hill near Bennington and practices. Holding
his glider kite, Dave runs down the slope into the

oncoming wind. When he moves the control bar forward, he sometimes rises into the air. When that first happened, Dave forgot everything he had been trying to learn and stared at the ground a few feet below him in total disbelief. "It blew my mind," he said. "I was off the ground. I was flying!"

In this country, the sport of hang gliding got its

start in California around 1970. The high cliffs overlooking the westward-facing beaches proved to be good launching sites. Since then, hang gliding has become a truly national sport. The USHGA (U.S. Hang Gliding Association), a growing and spirited body, is the national organization. A division of FAI (Federation Aeronautique Internationale) represents hang gliding on a worldwide basis and claims members from Australia to Austria, where the first World Championships were held in 1976. More than 12,000 members belong to one or the other of these organizations. According to the USHGA, more than 100,000 people have tried the new sport.

Hang gliding attracts people of all ages and from all walks of life. Michael McCarron, of Saratoga Springs, New York, has taught hang gliding for over two years. His students include teen-agers, grandfathers, skiers, musicians, and his wife.

To many spectators and journalists, the sport appears to appeal to daredevils only. And of course, there are fliers who delight in acrobatics and competitive stunts. But these pilots make up only a small fraction of those who fly, first from the slopes of hills and then from cliffs or mountaintops.

It is little wonder that spectators get the feeling of daredeviltry when pilots step off cliffs or leap from mountain outcroppings with their gliders. The sight of people in their gliders, high above a valley

A pilot steps from a mountaintop and "flies like a bird."

floor, is a breath-stopping thing to watch. It also stops traffic, as it did when hang gliders were seen taking off from Yosemite National Park's Glacier Point, over 3000 feet above the valley floor. The tiny specks in the sky above the spectators were men, flying like birds. Cars stopped. Tennis games stopped. Boats on the river stopped. Everything stopped, as people watched the "daredevils."

How do these daredevils feel, as they move out, away from the cliff and into the air? John Davis, who made a Yosemite flight, described it beautifully. "You're still breathing hard from that first takeoff from the edge of the world. It's amazing how the ground just seems to drop away from you—10 feet, 50 feet, 200 feet, and finally over half a mile. But now you are caught up in the sheer natural beauty that envelops you from all sides. Yosemite Falls fractures the rays of the morning sun as it wakes from its resting place behind Half Dome, creating a million little rainbows, for which hang glider pilots have the exclusive vantage point. Your distance from the valley floor miniaturizes the rivers, lakes, trees, buildings, and cars. People are too small to be seen. All the intricate maneuvers you had planned for the high-altitude flight were left on takeoff, as you spend your 14 minutes of flight looking at the living painting from an angle that few people are privileged to experience. You notice that you are talking to yourself and trying to keep from shouting out loud how you feel. Five minutes into the flight your face starts to ache because you can't stop smiling. Now, over the landing area at 2000 feet, the air is so smooth that you can, for the first time, check your kite's handling. You can begin to wonder how many 360s you could spiral off before landing. People begin to appear beside the houses and cars. You don't want to come down, but the lack of thermals in the early morning makes it a necessity. In fact you are rapidly approaching the tops of the trees; your landing approach may be your easiest, but you can't relax. The meadow is about a quarter-mile

6

square, so with the cool early morning sink in the meadow, you just pull it in at treetop level and come in for that final ground skim to a landing so soft that your feet don't even leave footprints on the thick, long meadow grass.

"Two little old ladies rush out to ask if they can take your picture to show the folks back home, and you are still so naturally high from the flight that you couldn't care less. Folding up your kite, you see your friends landing around you and you can see the same thing in their faces that you feel in your own. Nothing needs to be said, so you just stand there, grinning at each other."

The feeling that John Davis had has little to do with daredeviltry. The feeling of oneness with the environment that all hang pilots experience does not square with many people's view that hang gliding is some expression of an imagined "death urge." It is, more accurately, a "life urge."

Many of the veterans of this new sport are in their late teens or in their twenties. Many of these young people are instructors, and they often teach the rules of hang gliding to would-be pilots more than twice their age. But the common bond of being able to fly like a bird wipes out all age differences.

Old and young people alike are launching their gliders now from Torrey Pines, California; from Lookout Mountain in Tennessee; from Mt. Greylock, in Massachusetts; and from the sand cliffs of Wellfleet, on Cape Cod. And hundreds more will follow them. Observers of this growing (or exploding) sport naturally wonder how it all began.

2
The Birth
of Hang Gliding

In 1936, Francis Rogallo was working as an aeronautical engineer for the Langley Research Center in Hampton, Virginia. At that time he was testing airplane wings in wind tunnels to find out which shapes gave the most lift to a plane. With his mind on wings, Rogallo began to wonder whether a simple piece of cloth attached to a frame could sail like a kite if the air pushed out the cloth to form a wing like those he had been testing.

The airplane wings he tested every day were shaped with ribs to form curved surfaces. The air flowing over the fixed, or rigid, wings produced lift for the plane. But, Rogallo asked himself, why couldn't a triangular-shaped kite billow up with the air pushing beneath it and produce a curved surface that would produce lift like a regular airplane wing? Rogallo tried it, and it worked.

He used his knowledge of aerodynamics (air in

motion) and his engineering skill to invent what is now called the Rogallo wing, or "kite." At first he wondered what he could do with his invention. He patented it, but nothing much happened. Then, when the National Aeronautics and Space Administration (NASA) came into being, Rogallo went to work for them. He offered NASA his invention on a royalty basis, if they could use it.

Some tests were made with Rogallo's kite, which was used as a kind of parachute to get space vehicles back into the atmosphere. The army found they could drop jeeps with it. But in the midst of the thousands of problems NASA dealt with, the Rogallo kite did not make much of an impression. Except for one thing, Rogallo's invention would have been forgotten: descriptions of the Rogallo wing were published in NASA's periodic reports and sent out to interested people.

One of those interested people was a man living in northern California, Barry Hill Palmer. When he saw the NASA report on the Rogallo wing, he bought materials and built one. Then, by running with it on the sand dunes along the Pacific, he made several short, soaring flights. Barry Hill Palmer is generally credited with being the first hang glider pilot.

Across the country in North Carolina, an engineer, Thomas Purcell, also read the NASA reports. He built a Rogallo wing, which was towed aloft by an airplane at a local airport. He is considered the first to fly a towed Rogallo.

Francis Rogallo invented the wing (sometimes called the Rogallo standard). Palmer was the first recorded pilot of the wing. But William Bennett, of Australia, really got the sport of hang gliding off the ground. As early as 1956, Bennett and his friend William Moyes were experimenting with a kite of their own invention: cloth stretched as tightly as possible over a winglike frame. They skiied furiously downhill with their kite, trying to soar aloft. They also tried to wing it behind motor boats, but the flatness of their kite wing made their glider unstable. They probably would have killed themselves if they had not tumbled into water or snow when the kite tipped over and fell to the ground. Then a friend of theirs from New South Wales received the NASA report on the Rogallo wing. Since the cloth on the Rogallo kite was loose, it filled with air and gave stability to the kite. Bennett and Moyes immediately built one and began soaring. They still got up in the air by being towed, but one day the towline broke. Bennett soared gracefully to earth. Soon both men had become able hang glider pilots. Bennett and Moyes came to the United States, where they startled a great many people. Bennett soared out over San Francisco Bay above the Golden Gate Bridge and landed on Alcatraz Island. In New York, he was

Wilbur Wright flew his early glider at Kitty Hawk, North Carolina, in 1902.

towed above the Statue of Liberty. After he was cut loose, he spiraled around it to the ground. He was also towed (and photographed in flight) behind motorboats in Florida. Then he jumped off a mountain over a mile high in California and glided down to land in Death Valley. His friend Moyes attracted attention when he jumped off the rim of the Grand Canyon and glided to the bottom.

Bennett, more than anyone else except Rogallo, helped give birth to the sport of hang gliding. It caught on rapidly on the West Coast and soon began to spread eastward. In recent years it has become a nationwide and worldwide sport. Even Francis Rogallo himself fell victim to it, and when he was in his early sixties, he took up the pastime at his retirement home near Kitty Hawk, North Carolina.

Kitty Hawk is more than the retirement home of Francis Rogallo. It is the place where the inventors of the airplane, the Wright brothers, made their first successful flights. They began with gliders, much as hang glider pilots are doing today.

Wilbur and Orville Wright were bicycle manufacturers from Dayton, Ohio. They read everything they could find about a German flying inventor, Otto Lilienthal. Lilienthal spent many years trying to realize his dream of man flying. He observed birds flying, and he tried to build a machine with wings that would flap and send him

Octave Chanute's glider was flown in 1897.

aloft. His machine is called an ornithopter. After years of effort, he realized that human muscles could never make the wings beat with enough force to lift a human body into the air. He turned his attention to gliders and made more than 2000 flights before he died in a glider crash.

The Wright brothers followed all of Lilienthal's experiments with a lot of interest. They also corresponded with another gliding pioneer, Octave Chanute, of Chicago. Both Lilienthal and Chanute observed the actions of models in flight and then tried to fly full-size gliders.

The Wright brothers found it necessary to practice continually in order for the pilot's body, which controlled the glider, to respond automatically to changes in flight. They knew this because they knew that was the way you learned to ride a bicycle or to drive a stick-shift car. If you tried to learn to drive a car by going out in it only once a month, your feet and hands would "forget" the motions practiced a month before.

Late in the summer of 1900, the Wright brothers took a glider to Kitty Hawk, North Carolina. They first flew it in a steady wind, like a kite, with the control wires held in their hands. Then they tried flying it with one of them as the pilot. They managed to fly, but not without much more wind than they had thought necessary. In 1901 they tested a larger, heavier glider. Its design was based on Lilienthal's and Chanute's scientific data. But it was less successful than their first glider.

During the winter of 1901-2, they abandoned the scientific data and did their own testing in a crude wind tunnel. At that point, both brothers had more continuous flying time than either Lilienthal or Chanute. They could, and did, remember the experience. In addition, they had developed a method of twisting the wingtips of their glider to keep the wings in level flight.

The wing-twisting control provided what is called lateral stability. If a gust of wind pushed the right wing down, they could twist the wingtips with control wires. The wind itself helped level the glider. The idea of twisting the wings is an example of the Wright brothers' practical approach to all the problems they met.

The idea came to Wilbur one day in his bicycle shop in Dayton. He had just sold an inner tube to a customer. As Wilbur stood talking to the man, he twisted the tube's cardboard box, first one way and then the other. Glancing down, he saw that he was warping the box ends—one end down, the other end up. A glider wing could be twisted the same way.

In the fall of 1902, the Wright brothers made hundreds of flights in a glider based on all their experiments. They had solved the problem of controlled glider flight.

The Wright brothers' work realized the centuries-old dream of flying like a bird—a dream that can be traced back to Greek mythology. A young man, Icarus, and his father, Daedalus, fashioned wings with bird feathers and wax to escape from prison on the island of Crete. According to the legend, they flew across the Mediterranean successfully, until Icarus flew too near the sun. Then the wax on his wings melted and sent him plunging to his death.

In the fifteenth century, Leonardo da Vinci made sketches of a wing-beating flying machine, or ornithopter, but it was never built. And no successful ornithopter has ever been produced.

Interest in gliders continued to grow, and in the early 1800s Sir George Cayley designed and tested gliders in England. He reported flights in 1809, and he continued to build and fly gliders into the 1850s. Another pair of American brothers, John and James Montgomery, built a glider in 1883 and flew it near San Diego, California.

All the pioneers—the Wrights, Lilienthal, Cayley, and the Montgomery brothers—worked on the problems of flight by using rigid-wing hang gliders.

Today credit goes primarily to the Wright brothers, who went beyond hang gliding by designing and constructing a glider with a gasoline engine and a propeller.

In so doing, they put hang gliding on the shelf

for fifty years. But in the process of their research and their gliding flights, they developed information about what makes a plane or a glider fly. They gave to the world the principles of flight, the same principles that apply to 747s and to the billowing wings of the A-shaped Rogallo kite.

All hang glider pilots today have to know and understand what those principles are. They must train their bodies to respond automatically to all types of winds and wind changes when they are flying—just as the Wright brothers learned to do so many years ago.

3
How Gliders Fly

When hang glider pilots step off a cliff or a mountainside, they start to fall. They and their gliders are heavier than air. But the glider wings are shaped so the pilots do not fall straight down. They and their gliders move forward as they fall. In other words, they glide.

Some gliders fall faster than others. To compare gliders, pilots use the term "sink" or "sink rate." This simply means that if a glider pilot steps off a 450-foot cliff and reaches the ground in 100 seconds, the pilot is sinking at the rate of 4.5 feet per second, and that is his sink rate. A glider that takes twice as long to fall the 450 feet has a 2.25-foot-per-second sink rate.

What makes the difference? The design and shape of the glider wing. Different wing shapes produce different amounts of "lift." Lift was one of the earliest discoveries in man's long quest to fly. It was found that if the upper surface of a wing

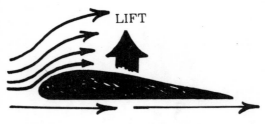

Air flowing over a wing produces lift.

curved upward, the air flowing over it bounced up and left a partial vacuum above the surface. Air pressure beneath the wing was then somewhat greater than the pressure above the wing surface. The difference in that pressure is the lift that helps keep a glider up.

Another critical thing about gliders is "drag." This is air friction, produced by air passing over all parts of the glider and the pilot. When drag slows a glider, air does not pass as rapidly over the wing. The lift is then reduced.

Wherever you go among hang glider pilots, you will hear them talking of the sink rate and the lift-drag ratio, because these things determine how efficient their gliders are. Pilots also use another phrase: "angle of attack." This means that if the front, or leading edge, of a wing is tipped up, the angle between the wing and the glider's flight path is the angle of attack.

What happens when a wing is tipped up, increas-

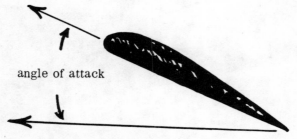

angle of attack

The angle of attack is controlled by the pilot.

ing the angle of attack? First of all, the lift is increased, which is good. But the amount of drag is also increased, because more of the wing's underside is exposed to the air. If the wing is tipped up too much, the wing will "stall." When this happens, all, or nearly all, of the smooth airflow over the wing's top surface stops. The lift then disappears, and the glider can fall like a stone toward the ground.

How Lift Is Created

The Wright brothers chose the sand dunes of the North Carolina coast to practice on because reports showed that there often was a strong, steady wind coming in from the sea. This, they reasoned, would allow them to hold the glider and run into the wind or down a sand dune and create enough lift to let them glide free of the ground. Within the limits of their wing design, they were correct. But the design data they first used were so poor that they had to

To create lift, a pilot runs down a slope.

mount the glider and its pilot on a track and have a cart tow them forward to get enough lift to let them glide.

Today hang glider pilots make use of the wind in the same way. If there is only a little wind, they have to run down slopes to create the airflow over the wing surface. If the air is not moving at all, they simply run faster in order to create lift.

One of the hardest things for many beginning hang glider pilots to learn is handling the wind. In fact, that is the main problem of flying a glider. The secret to staying aloft is flying the glider so that enough lift is created. The angle of attack varies the airflow over a wing. This determines the lift on a particular design. If a pilot increases the angle of attack too much, speed is lost. And if the air does not flow fast enough over the wing, the lift is lost. When that happens, the glider is in a stall. If it is a flexible wing kite, the wing will flap or invert (billow down instead of up). The only way to recover from a stall is to pull the nose of the glider down. The glider will immediately fall, but as it falls it will pick up speed and begin to create more lift. As speed is gained, the pilot brings the nose of the glider up slowly until it is at flying level again. Of course he has to have enough altitude to do this. If the glider stalls close to the ground, the pilot will crash before he picks up enough speed to restore the necessary lift.

The problem of flying downwind is that beginning pilots may not realize how much altitude they are losing. This has been the cause of many accidents, some of them fatal. It is easy to see, on paper, why downwind flying is dangerous. It is another thing for a pilot to remember it when he is flying.

If, for example, a pilot is standing on the edge of a sand dune ready to launch against a 15-mile-an-hour wind, the glider already has some lift on the wing—15-miles-an-hour worth, to be exact. When the kite is launched, it begins to fall. The air underneath the wing slants the kite forward so it doesn't fall straight down. The pilot glides at a certain angle, depending on the design of the glider. By launching the kite, the pilot has begun to "fall" forward into the wind. If the pilot and glider travel at 10 miles an hour away from the sand dune, they are passing through the air at the effective rate of 25 miles an hour. This creates plenty of lift to fly comfortably. But now let us say that the pilot is going to turn downwind or fly in the direction the wind is going. The wind is behind the pilot. It no longer creates lift. To keep the same lift on his wing, he must increase his sink rate.

Controls

Rogallo gliders, or standards, have flexible wings

The control bar lets a pilot guide his glider.

like sails. They have no movable controls like those on ordinary airplanes. How then can hang glider pilots maneuver their gliders? They do it by shifting their bodies around. This in turn changes what is called the center of gravity.

Every object or combination of objects has a single point at which gravity can be thought to act. If you put your finger at the proper place along a baseball bat, for example, it will balance. That is its center of gravity. Hang glider pilots harnessed in their gliders have such points. When the pilots move their bodies, they shift the center of gravity, and the gliders tilt one way or the other.

The Rogallo standard has a control bar—a large triangle of aluminum tubing fixed to the glider frame. Pilots use this to pull themselves forward in the harness or to push themselves backward. If they pull themselves forward, the nose of the glider tips down and, in the air, the glider gains speed and loses more altitude. If they push themselves from the control bar, toward the tail, the tail tips down and the nose tilts upward. The glider gains lift and loses speed.

To turn, pilots move their bodies in the direction they wish to turn. The glider tilts that way and begins a turn. So by moving their bodies, hang glider pilots maneuver their gliders.

More advanced gliders, with rigid wings, are designed with some movable controls, so that by using a combination of body movements and the controls, pilots can maneuver themselves in flight.

Turns

To turn a glider, the pilots of Rogallo standards must shift their weight and "tip" their gliders over slightly. But once they have tipped them enough, they must get their weight back in the center again or else the gliders will go on tipping steeper and steeper until they stall and spin. When the pilots have tipped or banked the glider enough, they are in a turn and can continue that turn as long as they like. But all the time they are in a turn they are losing altitude, because the lift on their wings is reduced when the wings are banked, or tipped. If pilots have plenty of altitude, they do not mind losing some of it. But if they are near the ground, the amount of altitude they lose can be critical.

Since a glider in a turn has reduced lift, it is necessary to put the nose down a little to increase speed and produce more lift. But this, too, causes a loss of altitude.

Landing

Landings are the most difficult maneuver pilots have to make. Taking off is easier for the simple reason that pilots can stand on the ground and judge everything before they launch their gliders. They have time to think things through. In landing, however, there are only fractions of seconds in which to make judgments, figure out what to do, and do it. As far as the glider is concerned, it will stop moving forward when all lift is destroyed—in other words, when it is completely stalled and the uniform wind flow over the upper surface is interrupted. If the glider stops moving forward and all lift is destroyed, it will fall, straight down at first.

To land a glider, then, pilots try to accomplish two things: stall their gliders at exactly the moment they plan to; and have their feet touch the ground at that instant.

4
Glider Country, Glider Winds

Hang glider pilots are always looking for something they can't see: wind. Moving air can be felt, and its effects can be seen. But the moving air itself remains invisible. And as hang glider pilots gain more and more experience, their senses are sharpened, and their minds take notice of many things nonflyers do not pay attention to: the slope of hills and ridges, the formation of clouds, the flight of soaring birds, and more. They gradually learn about wind, what causes it, how to find it, and how to stay out of dangerous, turbulent air.

Causes of Wind

All of us live at the bottom of a sea of air. It is about 100 miles deep. Walking around on the earth, we are at the bottom of that sea. At times the sea of air is motionless over a large land area, much as it was that early morning in Yosemite when John Davis stepped off Glacier Point in his hang

Waiting for wind.

glider and glided down to the valley 3000 feet below. But unless hang glider pilots have a mountain to step off, they cannot fly in motionless air—they cannot stay in the air more than a few minutes. So they look for air in motion.

The main cause of wind is the sun. Its heat penetrates the sea of air, and its rays strike the earth, heating it. This in turn heats the air near the earth's surface. That heated air expands, and as it expands, it rises. Cooler air, surrounding the warmed air, fills in the space below the rising warm air, thus producing air in motion, or wind.

A good example of this can be found on the coast of California, where hang gliding in the United States got its start. When the sunlight heats up the land along the coast, it heats the air above the land, and the air begins to rise. That same sunlight falls also on the water offshore. But water can absorb a lot more heat than land. As the water soaks up the heat, it does not reflect the heat into the air above it, so that air stays cold. Now, as the warm air over the land rises, the cold air over the water moves toward the shore to take the warm air's place. In other words, a wind comes from the sea to the beaches and cliffs that form the shore. So common is this kind of wind that it has been given its own special name: an onshore wind, or sea breeze. Using the onshore wind, hang glider pilots up and down the California coast stand on the cliff edges and launch themselves into the wind. At night the wind reverses itself, because the land cools off quickly when the sun has set, and the water, with the sun's heat still in it, becomes warmer than the land. Then the wind blows from the land out over the water. Near the end of the day, as the shift from onshore to offshore wind takes place, the changing winds are weak, and hang glider pilots must end their day's adventures.

So the sun, heating different surfaces unequally, heats the air above those surfaces unequally. It is this unequal heating, with the warmer air rising and the colder air flowing in beneath it, that causes the winds near the earth at the bottom of the 100-mile-deep sea of air.

This is also true away from the water. If, for example, a large forest is next to a large open space of earth, such as a farming area or a desert, the sun heats the two areas unequally. Air over the open ground heats up and rises, while the forest absorbs more of the sun's heat, leaving the air above it cooler. The cool air then flows across the open spaces to take the place of the air that has risen, and a wind is created.

All over the earth cold air slides under warmer air as warm air rises. Sometimes the amount of air in motion is huge. In winter, for example, great masses of cold air drift southward from the Arctic regions to replace equally large masses of warm air

RIDGE LIFT

Air moving over a ridge must rise, creating lift.

over most of the United States, as well as other air masses coming north from the hot equatorial regions in the Gulf of Mexico and the Caribbean Sea. Such large air movements cause winds for days over great areas of the country.

How Land Forms Shape the Wind

Hang glider pilots look for land formations that will make a horizontal wind move upward. There are many such shapes. The beach cliffs on the West Coast are a good example. As the sun-created wind moves shoreward, it runs into the cliffs and is pushed upward. Along the ridge of the sand cliffs, pilots find the air moving upward, like water flowing over an obstacle in a stream. Many other obstacles make a horizontal wind rise and flow over them. A line of hills, a large mountain, a row of trees, high fences, or a row of houses—all cause a horizontal wind to rise. Some of these land shapes make good rising currents for hang gliders to fly in. Others create a lot of scrambled air, like a wave breaking on a beach, and this kind of land shape is dangerous for hang gliders. In fact even with the best shapes—a low, even line of sand cliffs, for example—the air that is pushed up over the tops can then fall, or sink, behind the obstacle. A glider in sinking air is in a dangerous position, because not only is the glider going to fall of its own weight, it will also be carried downward faster by the sinking wind.

If the wind is strong and the slope of the cliffs steep, the wind rises strongly and then "breaks" like a water wave over the cliff tops, causing turbulence that cannot be flown in.

Flying in Ridge Lift

Spectators who watch hang gliders flying over the California sand cliffs have seen them glide along for great distances parallel to the cliffs without ever rising or sinking. Many wonder what keeps the gliders up. The answer is the rising wind flowing up and over the cliffs. If pilots can stay in air rising at 300 feet per minute while their gliders

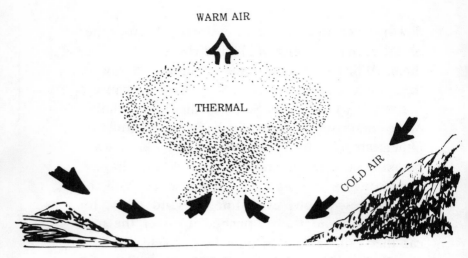

WARM AIR

THERMAL

COLD AIR

Over warmed ground, air heats and rises as thermal columns or bubbles.

are sinking at 300 feet per minute, they will not lose altitude. When pilots want to turn around and fly back along the beach, they turn into the wind to maintain the lift on their wings, lose a little altitude, and they try to regain it in the rising wind along the beach. If that rising wind is strong and the upward air movement enough to overcome the glider's natural sink rate, the pilot may gain some altitude.

Flying in Thermals

Hang glider pilots have recently learned to fly in thermals. What is a thermal? It is a bubble of warm air that breaks loose from the ground and rises through cooler air like a bubble of air underneath water coming up toward the surface.

Here is how Chris Wills, a veteran hang-glider pilot, describes his first experience flying in a thermal: "I was way out over the landing area and felt a bump that registered zero in my mind. I looked at my variometer [an instrument that tells glider pilots how fast they are rising or falling] and noticed that it said 500 feet per minute up. Doubting my sanity, I could feel nothing. I started to circle, looking only at my variometer. It continued to read 500 fpm up, so I made about ten turns—still feeling nothing. I then looked down at the ground and was amazed to find myself at least 1000 feet above takeoff and about 2000 feet above where I started. We had always talked about using thermals, but deep down inside I had never really believed you could gain any real altitude over flat ground in a hang glider. Two days after I had gotten my variometer, I had done it. I discovered I had been flying through lift for months without knowing it was there!"

One of the reasons Wills had not known before that he had frequently flown through thermals is that under many conditions glider pilots cannot know by observation whether they are rising or falling. It is like going up in an elevator at constant speed. There is no sensation of rising (except when the elevator starts and you feel it speeding up by the pressure on your feet). But Wills had just bought a variometer and fixed it to his control bar. Since his instrument was very sensitive and registered rising or falling, he had to believe his eyes when he watched it.

Of course, when more altitude has been gained, pilots can see that the ground is farther away. But that gain in altitude will occur only if the pilots stay in the thermal bubble. Before his experience with thermals, Chris Wills, like many other pilots, had flown straight through thermals. Other pilots had experienced the same bumps Wills reported. Those bumps are caused by moving from still or downward-moving air into the rising air of a thermal bubble. It is the kind of jolt you would get from stepping off a moving bus to a nonmoving street. Today hang glider pilots are trying to find thermals and are learning to fly in them.

Since thermals are limited in size, the pilots have to circle around and around in them, the way Wills instinctively did. They cannot see thermals, and so, again, they are looking for invisible things. Pilots have learned that most of the time thermals do not rise straight up. If there is a horizontal wind blowing over the area, a thermal bubble will drift with the wind as it rises. How then do pilots find thermals to fly in?

One way is to study cloud formations, for when a thermal with some moisture in its air rises high enough, the moisture condenses and forms a cloud. Another way is to watch soaring birds. Many species, such as swallows, fly in spiraling patterns in order to feed on insects carried up by thermals that started over the ground. One pilot has even learned to smell them. If he is gliding 1000 feet above the ground, and smells the scent of fir trees or smoke, or any other smell from the ground, he is sure that he is flying through a thermal.

What Thermal Soaring Means

Ridge flying—flying back ·and forth, back and forth along a ridge for hours—has become boring for many pilots. They look for new ways to fly. In thermal soaring, they have found a way to soar on long cross-country flights. (The poor car driver who has to pick them up may have to chase after them for hours.) Once in a thermal, or a line of thermals, the hang glider pilot can go from bubble to bubble (if he can find them) and gain altitude, which increases his ability to glide farther and farther across a desert or plain.

In fact, many pilots are now able to stay aloft for so long that fatigue is a problem. Constant alertness and muscular tension can make pilots very tired. Another problem is the temperature. As pilots go higher in the sea of air, they notice the falling temperature. If they are dressed for warmer weather on the surface of the earth, they can get

very cold several thousand feet up. This, in turn, increases fatigue. Still another factor that many pilots worry about is the thinning air, the lack of oxygen. If pilots take off at 3000 feet above sea level and climb in thermals 12,000 more feet upward, they are in a region where oxygen is scarce. If they are not careful, they can get more

Flying above the clouds can be dangerous.

than a little goofy from lack of oxygen; their judgment about when to come down can be seriously affected.

The future of experienced hang glider pilots is pointing more and more to thermal flying, cross-country flying, and altitude competition, for, as Wills has said, "Thermal soaring is far and away better than ridge soaring. In most thermal conditions, there is not the great wind associated with ridge soaring, so your freedom of travel is much less restricted. Thermal soaring is an intellectual process that offers greater satisfaction because it is more demanding of precise flying and thinking."

5

The Danger
in Hang Gliding

Since the 1950s, when Bill Bennett was towed above the Statue of Liberty and glided around it to its base, people have been talking about how dangerous hang gliding is. Magazines and newspapers have printed numerous articles about the hazards of the sport.

The fact is that any sport requiring individual physical effort can be dangerous. Rock climbing, skiing, scuba diving—all contain elements of danger. But somehow hang gliding has been falsely labeled "the most dangerous sport of all."

The U.S. Hang Gliding Association began collecting data on fatal hang gliding accidents on a worldwide basis several years ago. The association found that from 1971 through 1975 there were 110 known deaths. It was during this time that the sport of hang gliding was catching on. More and more people were trying to fly without proper training,

A pilot crash-landed in a tree.

44

and, of course, the number of accidents was skyrocketing, too. In 1974, for example, there were five times more fatal accidents than in 1973.

USHGA officials argue that hang gliding was growing so fast that proper training of pilots and self-policing were impossible. Then, in 1975, the number of deaths dropped. There were 14 percent fewer fatal accidents in 1975 than in 1974. The efforts of experienced pilots to train newcomers in the sport, and to set up training-school requirements, were paying off.

No amount of training will take the danger out of hang gliding, however. It is, and always will be, dangerous. Chris Wills, the hang-gliding veteran, says, "If you think hang gliding is perfectly safe, it can be dangerous. If you think hang gliding is dangerous, it can be perfectly safe." This is only partly true, since nothing is "perfectly safe."

The Sources of Danger

Automobiles, motorcycles, airplanes, speed boats, and hang gliders are driven by human beings, and human beings make mistakes. In hang gliding, it is the human being who is the greatest source of danger. The danger may come from a pilot's ignorance of flying principles—what makes a hang glider stay up and what makes it come down.

The danger may come from a pilot's emotion—feeling like a bird, a feeling of freedom. It may come from his so-called bravery in launching a glider when wind conditions tell his brain not to take off. Or danger may come from a pilot's poor judgment—his not realizing, for example, that attempting to land while flying downwind is asking for trouble.

The other two things that make hang gliding dangerous are equipment failure and changing weather conditions during flight. But in most cases, accidents caused by these two things can also be traced back to the pilot. Checking equipment before flying may have been done too casually, and not allowing for weather changes may take a pilot to his death because he did not include a margin of safety in his plans.

Examples of Mistakes

One pilot, who lived to tell about it, took off one day in high wind that was gusty and unstable. He flew out from his mountain takeoff point and felt the bumps that hit his glider. Since they weren't too strong, he began to feel adventurous and brave—dangerous feelings for a hang glider pilot. Suddenly a gust hit his glider and turned it half around. He set it straight on course again, away from the mountain, when suddenly, in about one second, the wind took him straight up 1000 feet.

During this time, the pilot had the control bar of the glider pulled in, in order to try to get the nose of the glider down and lose altitude. But the wind took him up anyway. Suddenly the wind flipped the glider upside down. He heard the aluminum frame crack. Then he was underneath the glider again, and falling. The broken glider was spinning down, and the pilot could do nothing about it. He saw a large mass of rock below and the broken glider was headed straight for it. All he could think of, as the glider fell, was that he shouldn't have taken off in the strong, gusty wind. He believed he was going to die.

But before he could hit the rock, the wind drove the broken, spinning glider into some trees. The pilot hit the trees, fell into some bushes, grabbed them, and held on. He had no idea how badly he was hurt.

His glider was a mass of wreckage, strewn far up the slope from where he had stopped skidding. All he could do was hang on to the bushes. He looked down at one leg. It was twisted in an unnatural way, and he knew it was broken. At first there was no pain, only numbness. But he knew the pain would come.

Fifteen minutes after he fell, a helicopter flew over looking for him. It circled low over the mangled glider wreckage, then flew away. He realized his flying suit was the same color as the brush he lay in and that he was effectively camouflaged.

Later he heard someone walking around in the underbrush up the slope from where he lay. He tried to yell, but the pain in his ribs and chest prevented him from calling out. All he could do was whistle. He kept whistling until the rescuer found him. An hour later he was hospitalized with a fractured left shoulder and a fractured leg.

He had fallen in his broken glider about 2000 feet, spinning toward almost certain death. Luck alone had kept him from striking the large rock mass on the mountainside. What caused his accident? Not the wind and not the broken glider frame, which was never designed to fly in such strong gusts. It was the pilot himself who had nearly killed himself. He made his mistake long before the glider flipped over. He had stood on the takeoff site for half an hour, debating whether or not he should try to fly in the powerful wind. He let his bravery overcome his judgment. He knows today that if a pilot stands for half an hour debating whether it is safe enough to fly, it isn't.

If the injured pilot ever flies again, he may remember the saying that is as old as flying itself: "There are old pilots, and there are bold pilots. But there are no old, bold pilots."

Another mistake that human beings make affects us all, whether we are fliers or not. That is the attempt to gain attention, to demonstrate our skill, to show off. Hang glider pilots are no exception.

In Colorado not long ago, a young, experienced pilot was flying his hang glider. On the ground below him stood several of his friends, who had never seen him fly before. The young pilot wanted to land near his friends, who were directly underneath him. In order to do that, he normally would have tried to make a 360-degree turn, or turn in a complete circle. He would have tilted, or banked, his glider into a turn and remained banked until he had completed the circle; while he turned, his glider would have lost altitude. But the young pilot completed one 360 and then another, losing more altitude and coming down closer to his friends, who were watching in admiration. Then he tried a third 360 turn. He banked the glider steeply. It lost too much lift. The wings began to flutter. The steepness of his bank increased. He began to spin, and he fell out of control while his friends stood there helpless as he crashed to his death.

The young pilot was only twelve years old.

Bruce Morton of Glendale, California, an experienced top-ranking pilot, watched a similar situation when a pilot he knew crashed and died. And he wrote that perhaps many hang glider pilots are active in the sport because they want attention. Bruce admits that we all want attention and says that he did not compete for world records for nothing. But he adds that the important thing is to be able to recognize that the desire for attention can and will get a pilot into trouble. He advises not to give in to the urge to show off. Showing off has probably killed more hang glider pilots than anything else.

Where the Hazard Is Greatest

Most fatal or crippling accidents occur close to the ground. Taking off and landing are the most critical maneuvers a hang glider pilot has to execute. Taking off from a sloping hillside in a steady wind appears to be safer than stepping off a cliff, and certainly such hillside takeoffs are the only way beginners are trained. But a sudden, unforeseeable gust of the wind that was steady a moment before can carry a glider upward, push the kite's nose up, and produce a stall. This will wipe out lift in an instant. Unprepared, the pilot may fall 10 or 20 feet to the ground. Stepping off a high cliff, on the other hand, means an immediate gain in altitude above the valley floor. And altitude means safety.

Landings are more dangerous than takeoffs. One reason is that on takeoff pilots are concentrating on the problems of flight and are not in the middle of the thrill of flight. Coming down after even a few minutes of flying, pilots can forget how hard the ground is; they can forget wind speeds and direc-

Landings can be dangerous. Here one wing has hit the ground.

tions; their eyes and responses have been lulled by observing the ground and passing objects from a distance. Movements appear slow to pilots when they have altitude. As they approach the ground, things seem to be moving faster. Pilots can over-control; their muscles may tense; they can mis-judge speeds and their nearness to the ground. As one veteran pilot said, "The most hazardous position to be in while flying is close to the ground and slow." He recommends that each pilot's landing approach speed should be the best speed for the particular glider design plus half the wind speed. In other words, a pilot should not be anywhere near stalling speed, but should fly the glider to a landing rather than stalling it and "dropping in." Dropping in from a foot of altitude is one thing; dropping in from 10 feet is quite another.

Flying High

As hang gliding skills increase, one of the great challenges to pilots is to see how much altitude they can gain. By using thermals, many pilots gain a great deal of altitude. But it may prove to be fatal.

For example, if a pilot takes off from a Colorado mountainside, 6000 feet above sea level, finds thermals, and gains another 6000 feet, he will be 12,000 feet above sea level. At that altitude the air is cold and there is less oxygen in it than at sea level. The pilot can begin to be affected by the lack of oxygen. This is called anoxia (without oxygen).

The danger in flying at such an altitude, in getting up there and flying for any length of time, is that the effects of anoxia begin so slowly that pilots don't realize it. They are not aware that their brains lack oxygen for the simple reason that the only thing that can tell them *is* their brain—the first part of their bodies to be affected by the lack of oxygen.

A curious effect of a slow withdrawal of oxygen from the brain is that it makes you feel good. You have no problems. You feel drowsy. This is not the state of mind to have when soaring in a hang glider 12,000 feet above sea level. Pilots up there need all their wits about them. But anoxia has already taken their wits away.

Flying Far

If pilots are on long-distance flights, even at moderate altitudes, fatigue can be a very real threat to their safety. They probably are dressed for the temperatures at ground level, perhaps on a desert or a warm beach. And even at moderate heights, the air temperature is noticeably colder. So, if they are not dressed for high altitudes, or if they suddenly find thermals and decide to go as far as they can, they place themselves in a very hazardous position. As cold and fatigue increase, their judgment becomes poorer.

The effects of fatigue, cold, and lack of oxygen do not necessarily kill pilots immediately. If they have the altitude and there is no turbulence, they appear to be flying beautifully. But when they try to land, all the harmful effects can add up. Their judgment is often affected, and they may fly too far, select a poor landing site, come in downwind, fail to notice ground hazards, or be unable to handle the air turbulence often encountered near ground level.

As more and more pilots aim for cross-country flights and try to set distance records, they are learning to dress warmly and to take along small tanks of oxygen. Above all, they prepare for the hazard of fatigue as best they can and plan their flights carefully. If thermals fail to develop or carry them where they had not planned to go, the smart pilots come down.

Total Personal Responsibility

One of the appealing things about hang gliding is that pilots flying gliders must be totally responsible for their moves and thoughts. One experienced pilot has said that most people probably never have to take total responsibility for what they do. But in hang gliding you must. You cannot depend on anyone else. You have to know and admit your limitations. You have to use your own judgment and cannot depend on anyone else's. The fact that other pilots are flying in doubtful wind conditions does not give a pilot the right to say to himself, "Well, they are doing it, so it must be all right." It *may* be all right for them, but is it all right for the individual pilot about to take off?

Both of the fatal accidents described in the first part of this chapter would not have happened if the two pilots had undertaken total responsibility, if they had been honest with themselves and had resisted the challenge and the desire to show off. Their failure to do so was fatal.

6
Competition

Competition in hang gliding is as fierce as it is in any other sport. But it is skill, not muscle, that determines who wins. Luck and the weather play a large part, too. A hang gliding meet lasts several days, and the weather can change from minute to minute throughout the entire contest.

The site of the 1976 U.S. Championship meet was Dog Mountain, Washington. The hang glider pilots who participated in it found that the weather caused a great many problems. There were rain and mist, shifting winds, and muddy ground. The pilots drew lots to determine the order of takeoff from the launch site, which was 1480 feet above a reservoir; the landing site was right next to the reservoir, a 350-acre site when the water in the reservoir is low.

A number of expert pilots were victims of the changing weather. There was mud on the launch site, and several pilots slipped on takeoff. Winds shifting around the mountain gave some pilots perfect launchings. But other pilots had bad launchings with no lift at all or cross-wind takeoffs that slowed them down as they adjusted to the unusual wind direction. And there were times when the rain and mist kept all competition at a standstill.

Hang gliders in competition are frequently placed in three classes according to design. Class I is the simplest glider. The most common design in this class is the original, or slightly modified, Rogallo kite. Class II includes any glider without a fixed trailing edge on the wing or a rear spar (metal or wood stiffener), and with no controls other than the control bar. The glider must be capable of being carried up the hill by the pilot and flown unassisted in ordinary conditions. Class III is commonly referred to as the rigid-wing class. It includes any hang glider that is launched and landed by the pilot's own feet and that needs only one assistant for takeoff under good conditions. Thus any glider in a lower class may compete in Class III flying.

The three classes are necessary because of the very different flight characteristics of gliders of different designs. In the few short years of the sport's history, more and more advanced designs have been built. Not dividing the gliders into classes would give unfair advantage to the more advanced designs and would not test the pilots' skills accurately.

A pilot flies figure eights in competition around pylons.

Judging Skills

In an official USHGA competition, such as the 1976 Nationals at Dog Mountain, the skills that are judged are carefully spelled out. They fall into three categories: maneuvering, distance flown, and landing accuracy.

To test the pilots' abilities to maneuver, pylons are set up. The number of turns around the pylons a pilot makes before he loses too much altitude and has to land gives the judges a measure of the pilot's skill and the flying ability of the glider. There is also a test called slow-flight maneuvers. The object of this contest is to see how many left and right 90-degree turns a pilot can make over a 100-yard course. It requires the pilot to fly slowly—just above the stalling speed of his glider. To make matters more difficult, the course is only 30 yards wide, and the pilot is not supposed to go beyond the sidelines.

The landing accuracy event is probably the most interesting one for spectators. The pilots try to land on a particular spot on the ground, an area no bigger than the first-base bag in a baseball game. In fact, the measured space, as designated by the USHGA Competition Committee, is even smaller than a first-base bag. It is a 4-inch-diameter center spot on the bag. Landing on it is much like trying to hit a small bull's eye. Points are taken away for the distance from the spot the pilot lands. The

A touch-down landing on the bull's eye.

Committee's rule is that a pilot loses 1 percent for every yard away from the center spot. Pilots who land outside the foul line score no points at all. Pilots are also penalized for unsafe landings. An unsafe landing is scored if any part of the pilot's body, other than the feet, contacts the ground during landing. An unsafe landing reduces the flight score by 50 percent.

In September, 1976, in Kössen, Austria, the first world hang gliding championships were held. The competition rules were slightly different from those used in most United States competitions. The rules for the world championships were made by the Federation Aeronautique Internationale (FAI) and the subdivision of that organization that sets the standards for hang gliding, the Commission Internationale du Vol Libre (the International Hang Gliding Commission).

Over twenty countries sent teams to Kössen for the 1976 championship competition. The pilots competed in two categories: time of the flight (with the pilot staying up the longest becoming the winner) and landing accuracy. The bull's-eye each pilot tried to hit was a circle 1 meter in diameter, which was in the center of a larger circle 50 meters in diameter. If pilots landed outside the 50-meter circle, they received no credit for the flight. They also got a zero score if they made unsafe landings.

The gliders were divided into three classes: (1) standard (like a Rogallo kite); (2) gliders with flexible wings and weight-shift control; and (3) open, or gliders of various designs.

For twelve days the pilots competed. When it was all over, world championships were awarded in each of the three classes.

The Weather Factor

Changing winds can frustrate competing hang glider pilots from the moment they take off. A wind that has been blowing directly at the launch site sometimes shifts just as the pilots' feet leave the ground. Their gliders, caught in a cross gust, can then stall and fall immediately. At best, such an occurrence forces pilots to lose altitude and make their flights shorter. Sometimes they are unable to reach the landing site and receive no points for their flight.

If pilots are going through slow maneuvers over the 100-yard course and the wind suddenly dies while they are in a turn, their gliders may stall and send them crashing to the ground.

The best judgment in the world can be useless when landing if a gust of wind suddenly comes from another direction. The change of wind can ruin the best approach a pilot can make. At the 1976 Nationals, for example, a veteran pilot, Bob Wills, fell victim to the weather. He had racked up high scores in all his flights and was well up among the leading scorers when a gust of wind hit his glider in his last turn to the target. He landed short of the foul line and lost all points for that flight.

During a takeoff in the same competition Jim Springer, of Tennessee, stalled his glider in a cross wind and crashed on a log-strewn slope just beyond the launch site. Later in the meet Scott Price, of Seattle, fell victim to gusts while flying his glider over the crowd toward the landing spot. He managed to crash-land between trailers parked nearby and escaped injury.

All of these mishaps were unpredictable. The pilots were all skilled fliers, but the changeable weather caused them to lose.

Cross-Country and Altitude Flights

At national and regional competitions, hang gliding pilots, their friends, and other spectators crowd together. Even while the competition is going on, the pilots who are not in it at the moment spend their time "free flying." Dozens of kites can be seen soaring on ridge lift and circling high above the landing place. Sometimes the pilots play "king of the mountain" to see who can soar highest on the lift, as the wind moves up and over the mountain where the meet is being held.

Trying to achieve cross-country or altitude records is another kind of competition. The pilots must find thermals to keep them aloft or, better still, a line of thermals that will let them soar for many miles and hours at a time.

When pilots set out on cross-country flights, they must have people on the ground to follow and track them, not to mention picking them up when they land. Sometimes this raises difficulties. If cross-country fliers lose the lifts that took them over strange territory, they may find themselves dumped on the ground among the hills. They then must walk back on their own.

This nearly happened to two veteran pilots. Trip

Mellinger and Rich Grigsby were gliding with some other pilots from a 1500-foot mountain in Sylmar, California. Most of their distance soaring before this flight had come from ridge lift along a line of hills. But on this particular day both of them noticed the formation of cumulus clouds over the mountains—a phenomenon that told them there was thermal activity going on.

Despite the fact that the day was warm, the pilots had brought along heavy clothing: winter underwear, parkas, and gloves. They knew that the temperature above the mountains was cold, and they wanted to fly there.

When they first took off, they could not find thermals, and they were rapidly losing altitude. Mellinger and Grigsby circled, looking for upward-moving thermals. When Grigsby was only 500 feet above the ground, he found what he was looking for. He felt a bump, then several more, as his glider stuck its nose into a thermal. He began circling, trying to define the thermal and stay inside it. A glance at his variometer showed him he was rising at more than 500 feet a minute. Trip Mellinger found a thermal, too. Soon the two pilots soared above the landing place and rose into the clouds.

Then both men quickly steered their gliders below the cloud base so they could see what was going on. By this time they had lost sight of one another. When Grigsby set out across the mountains, he was almost forced down for lack of lift. Then he spotted a hawk, circling and rising about 200 feet away from him. He immediately joined the hawk and sailed on up.

Sometimes in sight of one another and sometimes alone, the two fliers traveled over 20 miles before they came down. Rich Grigsby landed in a vacant lot next to a Howard Johnson's, startling the customers.

Both these flights were well documented and were entered in the records. Grigsby and Mellinger gained over 5000 feet of altitude; their height and distance became part of the record for others to shoot at.

Later in that same year Trip Mellinger and another friend, Gene Blythe, set a new distance record. They flew 47.2 miles in 2½ hours, following a line of thermals made visible by a forming line of cumulus clouds. During their flights, they rose for a few minutes to 14,500 feet above sea level. Both pilots suffered from severe cold and lack of oxygen, but when they returned to earth, they had the necessary records on their barographs to give them official standing. (Today, the USHGA requires verified barograph records for distance and altitude claims.) Both men believe that flights of 100 miles and more are possible if the human body can stand the strain.

Pilot with a backup system of oxygen tank and barograph.

The Barograph

The barograph is an instrument that measures time and air pressure. As time passes, its small drum rotates slowly. The drum has a paper graph on it and a moving marker that draws a line. Since the drum rotates at a slow but constant speed, its rotation measures the time of a flight. As hang gliders go up or come down, they pass through air that exerts different pressure. The higher the gliders go, the less the air pressure is. The line drawn on the barograph's drum then wavers up and down on the paper. The pressure is greatest at ground level, therefore the line gives an accurate record of a flight.

Before takeoff, a barograph is readied and sealed by an observer. When the pilot comes down, the observer checks the instrument to see if it has been tampered with. If it hasn't, then the pilot's distance and altitude can be entered for the record.

What Some Pilots Think of Competition

Unlike many other sports, hang gliding was not begun for the sole purpose of competing. According to many veteran hang gliding pilots, there is more satisfaction in not competing than in competing.

It is hard to think of a sport where competing is not the ultimate aim. Can you imagine a track star

Close-up of a sealed barograph.

running and not competing against another runner or a stopwatch?

In hang gliding, many pilots get all their satisfaction from the sense of freedom, the solitude of the sky, and the mastery of the wind. One pilot, when asked about contests, said, "Somehow the winner of a contest is considered to be the best flier, but most of the best pilots I have ever seen rarely win contests. Also, in too many cases, the winner of a contest is either a local flier or a flier who gets the best conditions."

Keith Nichols, the 1976 United States National Champion, believes that competitions are fun, but he thinks of them as conventions where everybody gets together to see old friends, to examine new glider designs, and to exchange flying talk and information.

Of course, there will continue to be competitions. There will be awards and cups and medals. But even during the tightest race for the medals and honors, all anyone has to do to get the feel of the sport is to watch the free-flying pilots soar over a mountaintop.

7
New Gliders and Tomorrow

When Francis Rogallo developed his wing, he had no idea he would be considered almost the creator of the sport of hang gliding. His simple kite, with its somewhat triangular sail, became the glider that all the early hang glider pilots used. It had a tubular, metal leading edge to the wing and a metal keel running straight back from the nose to form the "tail" of the kite. Above the keel, mounted vertically, was a metal post, from which cables were stretched to the wingtips, tail, and nose. This gave the frame some rigidity. Beneath the keel was the control bar and pilot's harness. Cables ran from the control bar to wingtips, nose, and tail. When adjusted, the wires, or cables, made the frame a fairly rigid structure. This hang glider became so widely used it soon dropped the name Rogallo, and became known as the standard, or kite.

The proportions of the Standard's sail varied

The Easy Riser design is a modern ultralight.

somewhat, and as time passed, more and more pilots and designers began tinkering with its design. In just a few years, a number of changes were made in the standard. Some pilots thought the wingtips were too pointy; they fluttered in sharp banks or turns and increased the risk of stalling and going into a spin. One of the first steps in design modification was to cut the wing's tip off, thus producing a truncated tip.

Then, to help the wing hold its desired shape, thin plastic or wooden strips, called battens, were placed on the wing. The wing at the tips was rounded, scalloped, and otherwise experimented with by dozens of designers. One designer, Dick Boone, was pondering the problems of wing design one day while he was driving home from a meet. A bird soared by. He noticed the shape of the bird's wingtip, and immediately had the idea of designing a hang glider more like a bird. He developed what is called the radial batten tip.

All of these alterations changed the flying characteristics of the gliders. Some changes improved one flying quality, some another. One change, for instance, increased lift and reduced the glider's stability at slow speeds. Other changes produced a better glider at low speeds but limited its lift or increased its sink rate.

The standard Rogallo was modified out of existence. The new gliders were given a new name, ultralights.

Still other designers began experimenting with fixed-wing ultralights. The wings became more and more like the wings of modern airplanes. Many of the gliders looked like the two-wing glider the Wrights had developed at the turn of the century. Some gliders, like the Icarus II, had two wings and rudders near the wingtips. Others, such as the Quicksilver C, had one wing and an extended frame behind the wing with a tail and rudder attached. It resembled an early airplane. Still other gliders had rudders and stabilizers mounted in front of the wings. And they had rigid wings. The

A Quicksilver ultralight looks like an early airplane.

flapping sail, with battens, gave way to an airplane wing with metal edges all around it and solid ribs that gave the wing its desired shape. These rigid-wing gliders weighed more than the kites, and required trailers to get them to the launch site. Some could not be launched by picking them up and running down a hillside. But they had the advantage of being able to fly in less wind than a standard kite required. They produced more lift, even though they weighed more. Kites weigh about 35 to 40 pounds, but some of the newer, rigid-wing gliders weigh up to 75 or more pounds.

These newer and heavier gliders may be the coming thing. Seen in flight at a distance, with the pilots in prone positions, the gliders give the appearance of airplanes or sailplanes. The chief difference is that the hang glider pilots are outside the aircraft. They are not enclosed in a cabin, and they still feel that they are flying "free as a bird."

Towing

The idea of towing a glider until it rises into the air is not new. Bill Bennett and Bill Moyes, the Australian "early birds," were trying out their own kite design as long ago as 1956. But the only way they could get up in the air was by skiing down a snow-covered slope or being towed on water skis behind a motorboat.

Now, with the increasing popularity of hang gliding, the idea of towing as a means of getting into the air is growing. Many states have few, if any, hills or mountains high enough to be good launch sites and no line of cliffs to generate ridge lift for hang gliders. The plains of the western states and the farming states of the Midwest are flat for thousands of square miles. Both these sections of the country generate a lot of thermal currents, which could allow a lot of flying for hang-glider enthusiasts, but about the only way a hang glider can get up to catch the thermals is by being towed.

There are hazards in towing a glider aloft from the surface of the ground. Australian Bill Bennett, now heading his own company manufacturing

After cutting loose from a tow line, a pilot lands in the water.

hang gliders and tow-kiting equipment, has developed machinery that can tow gliders aloft over land. He claims his equipment will be the perfect thing for desert flying. Bennett's equipment consists of a pair of drums and a special combination of levers, sprockets, chain, and drums. You simply back a car's rear wheels onto the two drums, start the engine, and put the car in gear. The car's engine powers the towing mechanism at any desired speed.

Towing a glider aloft as high as 1000 feet before releasing can put hang gliders in thermals that will keep them up for long flights in the flattest part of the country.

Engines in Gliders

The only other way hang gliding pilots can get in the air in flat country is by using an engine to get off the ground. And even in country with hills or ridges there are days when the wind does not blow at ground level.

One young pilot, Chuck Catto, wanted to try an engine in a hang glider. He was a college student at the time and had had a little experience with sailplanes and with a standard kite. He had heard of an earlier experiment in which an engine had been used with an Icarus II, so he and his younger brother Craig bought an Icarus II and began experimenting with engines and propellers. The engine the brothers used was a 12-horsepower McCulloch. The next problem was the propeller. Chuck and Craig first studied propeller designs in handbooks, then set to work to build their own propeller. Their father helped, and when they had built a propeller 21 inches long, they tested it. It didn't work. Craig tried to take off with it, but the Icarus II with the McCulloch engine and their homemade propeller couldn't make it. After more study a second propeller was built, but it could not do the job they wanted it to do. By this time, Craig was getting used to making propellers. Chuck designed a third one, and his brother built it quickly. This propeller worked. The Icarus II could actually take off from level ground. The Catto brothers now take their Icarus II anywhere they wish. They start their engine and, with no wind at all, take off in less than 50 feet and climb at the rate of 150 feet per minute.

Someone once said, "They'll reinvent the air-plane if they're not careful." The aim of putting an engine aboard a hang glider is not to reinvent the airplane but to get the hang glider off the ground and up into bird country. Once they are up and flying, the Catto brothers turn off their engine and glide as true hang glider pilots. They have no desire to become power-plane pilots.

Future Threat and Future Promise

If an engine is placed in a hang glider, the glider

becomes an airplane. The Catto brothers realized this, and they knew that the Federal Aviation Administration had rules about where and how an airplane can be flown. The brothers obeyed the FAA regulations. But what bothers the leaders of the U.S. Hang Gliding Association most is that the FAA or some other government agency may try to regulate the entire sport of hang gliding. They know that sometime, somewhere, a hang glider and an airplane will collide in midair. Then, as one of the USHGA leaders says, "no matter who is at fault, the government will step in."

Some sports, such as tennis, bicycle racing, and scuba diving, have been successful without government regulation. Why, some people ask, should hang gliding be different? It is different because hang gliding attracts attention, because there have been accidents many have heard about. Magazines and newspapers have had stories in them about the "dangerous" sport of hang gliding. The same magazines and newspapers print stories of other sports where danger is always present. In hockey, in boxing, in car racing, in sky diving, there is danger. There is, in fact, danger in driving a car, standing in a shower, or crossing the street. But because hang gliding has gotten the name of "dangerous sport," the fear is that the government may decide to tell hang glider pilots when, where, and how they may fly.

Today, light-plane pilots are severely restricted

Hang pilots want
to remain "free as
a bird."

by the government. USHGA leaders know this, and worry about it. Another cause for their concern is the problem of safe design. The Hang Glider Manufacturers Association (HGMA) is trying to enforce structural standards for glider manufacture. When the sport was young, many "build-your-own-glider" plans were sold. Many people built gliders with whatever materials they could get. This produced a lot of dead hang glider pilots. The HGMA is now working hard to develop and enforce standards of construction that will keep the government out of the sport of hang gliding.

The USHGA has developed ratings for hang glider pilots so that dangerous launch sites will not be open to inexperienced pilots. There are five ratings, four of which are carefully spelled out. A pilot going to a dangerous site must show his rating certificate before he is allowed to use the launch point. And there are glider designs that will be sold only to experienced, capable pilots with the proper ratings.

These ratings are aimed at self-regulation for the sport. And for hang gliding self-regulation is extremely important, for what may seem like a strange reason—the type of person attracted to hang gliding in the first place.

What kind of people are hang glider pilots? There are many words that have been used to describe them. One of the most common is "individualists." Others are "misfits" and "non-belongers." To some extent, those words are accurate. Some pilots belong to various professions. Some work for corporations, others are self-employed. They are old and they are young. How can they all be "misfits?"

If the leaders of the sport of hang gliding are successful, they will avoid government regulation. Then the freedom-seeking, nonjoiners will be allowed to go on trying to find themselves.

They will launch their gliders. The earth will drop away. They will be entirely responsible for their lives. They will make the right moves, master the wind, use their brains and their judgment—*and* survive. Free as a bird.

NOTE: For further information on hang gliding, its equipment, and its training requirements, write:

The United States Hang Gliding Association
Box 66306
Los Angeles, California 90066